THE BOOK OF F*CKING HILARIOUS INTERNET MEMES

Richard Face

WATERBURY
PUBLISHERS

Cover Designed by: Damon Freeman

Typesetting by Kiersten Lief

Published by: Waterbury Publishers, Inc.

www.waterburypublishers.com

Visit the author's website:

www.internetmemebook.com

WTF IS THIS SHIT?

WHAT THE HELL IS AN *INTERNETMEME*?

Meme (pronounced *meem*):An idea, belief or element of social behavior spread that is transmitted from one person or group of people to another.

This word was coined in the '70s by Richard Dawkins, the atheist godman worshipped by neckbeards everywhere.

Simply put, Internet memes are memes that spread on the Internet through social networking sites, blogs, email, news sources, and so on. In the real world they're called "ideas," but pseudo-intellectuals prefer "memes."

WHERE DO INTERNET MEMES COME FROM?

Amongst all the stupid shit on the Internet are hilarious gems of wit and wisdom. Most of the best memes start as images shared on the Web and, by some great misfortune, they find their way into the lecherous hands of drunken basement trolls who mutate these images into the hilarious, the lame, and sometimes the downright bizarre.

WHAT IS THIS BOOK?

This book is a collection of the funniest memes I could find wading through the filthy bilges of the Internet. I wasted countless hours of my life just so you can have a good laugh, so be grateful motherfucker.

I hope this book makes you laugh. If it doesn't, it's probably because you have a shitty sense of humor.

THANKS TO ME & YOU
BECAUSE WE'RE FUCKING AWESOME

This book is basically a bunch of shit I jacked from the Internets and can't take any credit for beyond my greedy drive to capitalize on others' wit, which makes me awesome.

"Bad artists copy. Great artists steal."

Pablo Picasso

You were amused enough by this dumb idea to buy my book, which instantly makes you awesome.

So, without further ado, let's get this circus freak show started.

FOUL BACHELOR FROG
HE'S WORTH HIS WEIGHT IN PUBES

Foul Bachelor Frog is a heart-warming tribute to all the degenerate bachelor scrubs out there that live disgusting lives of self-abandonment and hopeless depravity. Not that this lifestyle doesn't have its perks, though. There's something oddly gratifying about playing PS3 at 4 AM in the nude while snacking on pizza rolls and going so long without a shower that your entire body smells like a sweaty nutsack.

Science has shown that males are genetically programmed to commit atrocities of hygiene and thus pretty much every guy between the ages of 18-35 has indulged in quite a few of those featured in this meme. Yes, your boyfriend/husband was/is a vile pig.

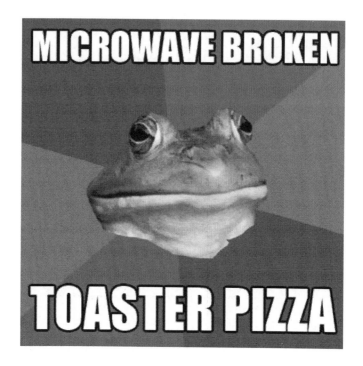

SOCIALLY AWKWARD
PENGUIN
I HERP WHEN I DERP

Some people just aren't made for human interaction. They get called by four different names and answer to them all, they tell jokes and forget the punch lines, they play along with stories even though they have no fucking clue what's being talked about.

But we can all relate to them sometimes. We've all had moments of social derp that we could giggle at without feeling compelled to immediately leave and rearrange our collection of bottle caps. Who hasn't missed social cues and acted like a fuck-up? Let he who hasn't mumbled like an idiot about shit nobody cares about cast the first stone.

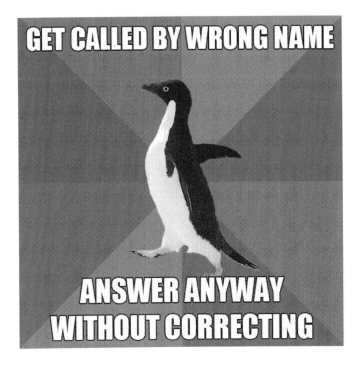

ADVICE GOD
LOL U MAD BRO?

While smug atheists and Yahweh fan boys continue to argue over some serious fucking business regarding a Jew wizard who lived 2,000 years ago, I have a more important theological question:

If God exists...is he the biggest troll in the universe?

This profound question occurred to me as I was reading the Bible, an epic chronology of God's Godly Adventures and the ultimate volume of trolling, extreme violence, incest, rape, and other hood ass shit.

By the end of this chapter you may not worship God for His omnipotent manliness, but you won't be able to resist his lure as the bossiest troll in da club.

CHILDREN EAT APPLE

4,000 YEAR GRUDGE

SNAKE TEMPTS MAN

KILL ALL THE DINOSOURS

MAKE SEX AWSOME

CREATE STDS

CREATE BLACK PEOPLE

LOL SCAPE GOATS

BORN IN NON-CHRISTIAN COUNTRY

DOOMED

FAIL TO MENTION DINOSAURS IN BIBLE

PUT FOSSILS EVERYWHERE

LOVE EVERYONE
KILL FAGS

JEWS ARE MY CHOSEN PEOPLE
HOLOCAUST

BAN SEX BEFORE MARRIAGE

IMPREGNATE UNMARRIED VIRGIN

HELP ACTRESS WIN AWARDS

DO NOTHING ABOUT WORLD HUNGER

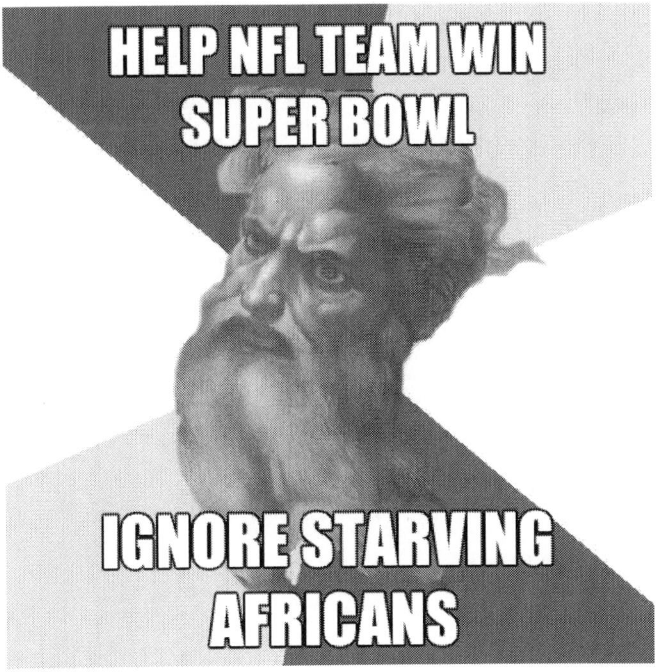
HELP NFL TEAM WIN
SUPER BOWL
IGNORE STARVING
AFRICANS

COURAGE WOLF
EAT LIGHTNING, SHIT THUNDER

Legends hold that Courage broke Odin's face and escaped from Valhalla to finish his work here on Earth, but there is much mystery surrounding his beginnings.

Every day of Courage Wolf's historic, awesome life is filled with badassery and win. His blood type is WD-40. He lets cops off with warnings. When he donates blood, he uses a handgun and a bucket.

Courage Wolf's mission is to bring hope and inspiration to the masses, and he's getting pretty damn e-famous for it. If you're ever feeling down or unsure of yourself, you can turn to this BAMF for guidance and inspiration.

PTSD CLARINET BOY
SOME THINGS...THEY JUST CAN'T BE UNSEEN

PTSD Clarinet Boy was once a happy young chap, but his now-grim face reveals an unthinkable trauma that shattered his fragile psyche. Haunted by horrific images of wanton death and destruction wrought by his hands while serving in a Special Forces kill squad, he can no longer feel the warmth of love or light of the world.

He has tasted human flesh; he hears voices in his head and they demand blood sacrifices; he can play a song for every man he has killed; he has counted to suicide and emerged unscathed; he believes he has become Death himself, the destroyer of worlds.

All he has left of his humanity is his clarinet and memories of the better times...

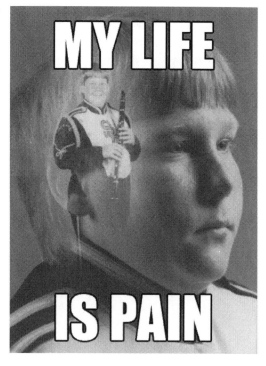

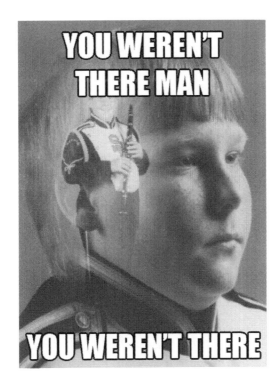

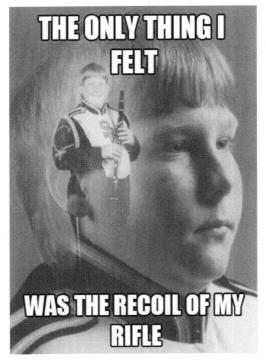

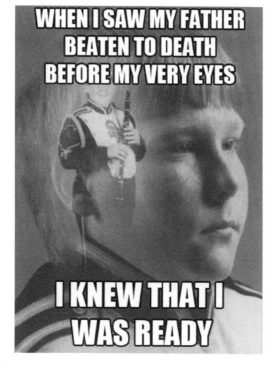

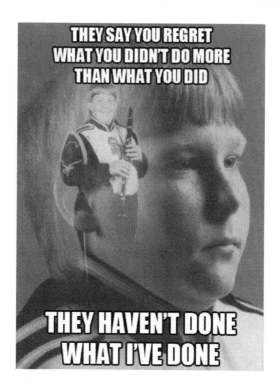

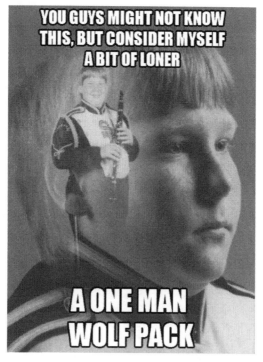

PARANOID PARROT
WHO SENT YOU THIS BOOK!?!?!

INCOMING TRANSMISSION FROM PARANOID_PAR-ROT69:

"I've been trying to get a message through to you for months now. Ever since I sent you the secrets revealed by evil Microsoft's Wingdings font, you've been under surveillance. In fact, your neighbor's dog is robot with x-ray scanning capabilities and his barks are transmissions to the grays orbiting Earth.

"The good news is you're coming close to the truth about the Masonic Jews and reptilian shape-shifting aliens, but the bad news is that your life is in grave danger. According to my sources, you will soon suffer an unfortunate accident involving a rapid chimpanzee and cocaine.

"There is but one solution: lock yourself inside, keep peanut butter smeared over your entire body, wrap your genitals in tin foil, and work on the 4th dimension equations I left at the drop location.

"Good luck and Godspeed. The fate of mankind rests in your hands."

END OF TRANSMISSION

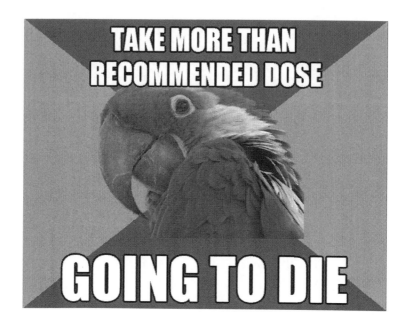

JOSEPH DUCREUX
DETRACTORS GONNA DETRACT

Joseph Ducreux was a French painter who painted people, fruit and shit back when France actually was semi-important and not just another gay European tourist trap. Ducreux specialized in portraits of snobby wannabe Jews like Marie Antoinette and her pussy husband Louis XVI, but that ended quick when all the French royals died by surrendering and being decapitated (which is the French tradition of how to end violent conflicts).

Ducreuxwas hardlyinterested in the finer points of being an artist. His self-portraits revealed his real nature: a straight OG baller that kept his pimp hand strong.

Due to his lifestyle of squandering his talent to get drunk and chase bitches all over Europe, the Internets realized that Ducreux would be a rapper if he were alive today. Thus the meme was born and it features Ducreux rapping modern hip-hop songs with 18th-century cracker flair.

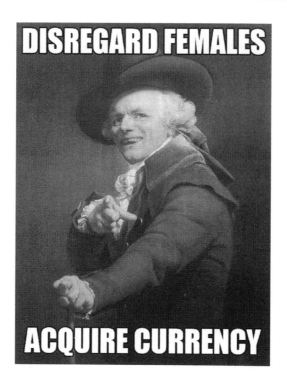

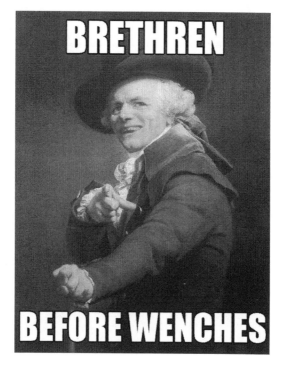

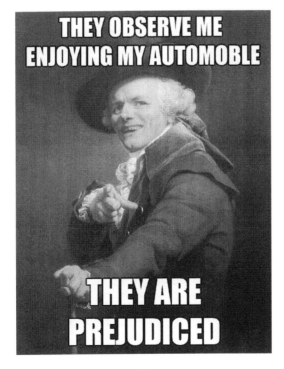

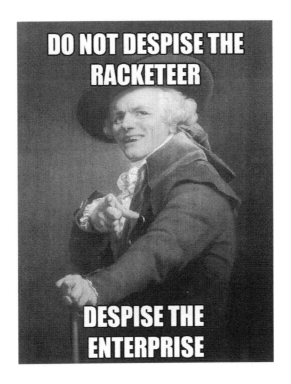

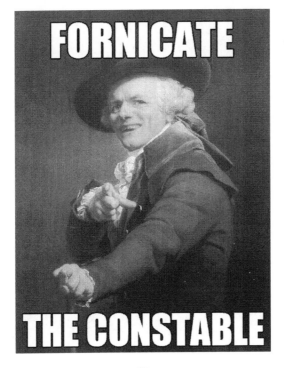

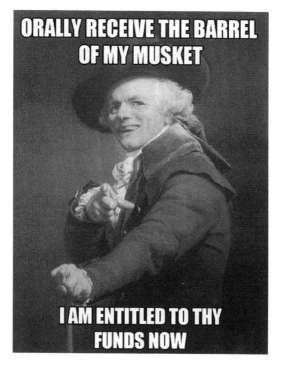

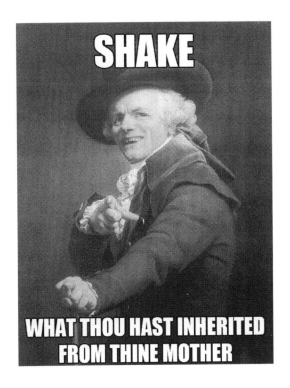

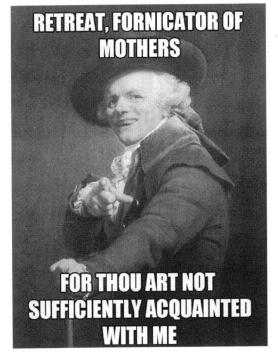

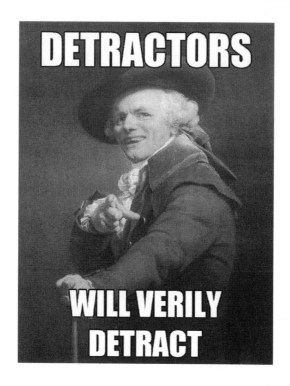

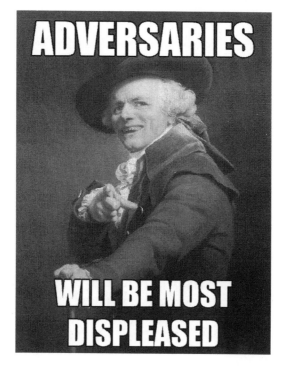

BEAR GRYLLS
I'D RATHER BE DRINKING PISS

Bear Grylls is a real fucking man who has a show that follows his ridiculous adventures of raping nature in the ass for ratings and lulz. This beast ravages anything that gets in his way, whether they are snakes, lizards, gazelles, or anything else dumb of enough to make eye contact with this insane motherfucker.

His show follows a simple formula: 1) get dropped off in a random place; 2) ensure 5-star hotel is within jogging distance; 3) eat innocent animals for lulz; 4) tell ridiculous story as to why he needs to snack on some elephant shit and proceed to snack on said shit; 5) wash shit down with some of his own piss; 6) ???; 7) profit.

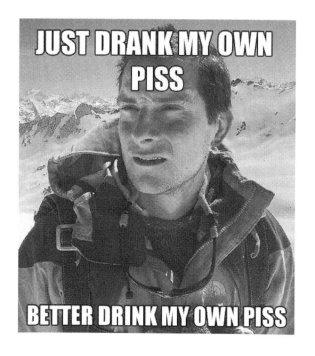

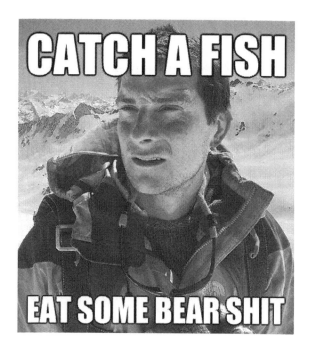

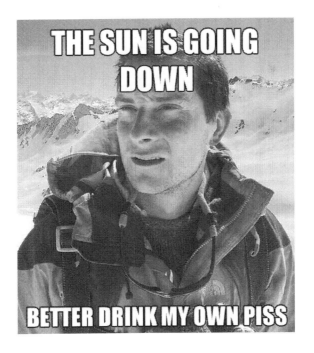

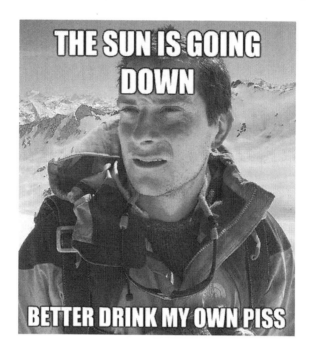

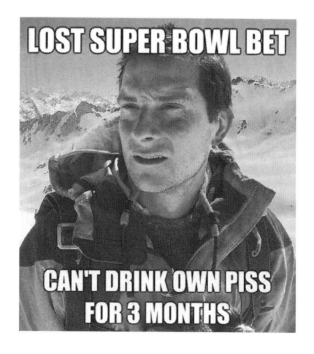

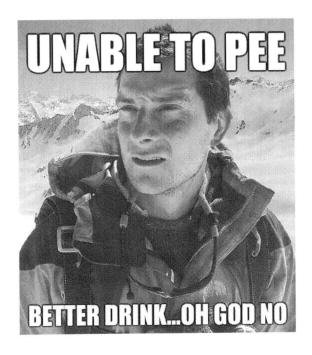

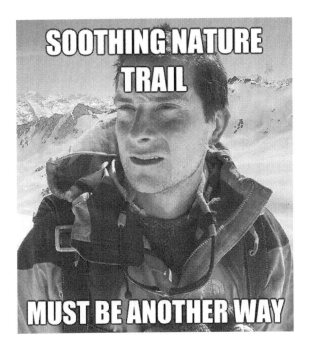

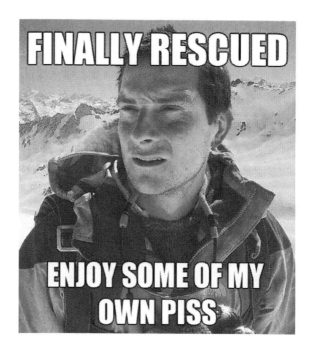

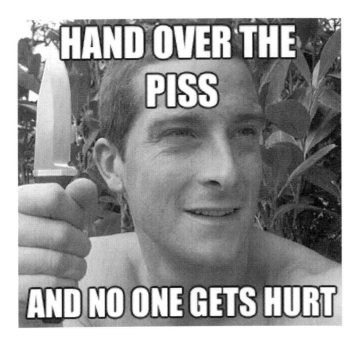

DOGFORT
I LOVE DOG

Dogfort is an Internets comic strip that features some epic dogs dressed up like all kinds of weird shit and usually fighting wars against cats. Dogs are cute. Dogs in costumes are super cute. Enjoy some fucking comics.

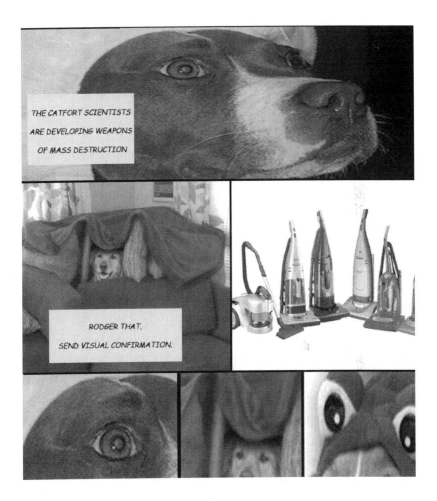

FOREVER ALONE
HIS LIFE PROBABLY SUCKS MORE
THAN YOURS

Forever Alone Guy (F.A.G.) is a rare type of social retard that dwells in an apartment or basement full of Pocky wrappers, pizza boxes, and cheap anime figures. He usually suffers from excessive fatness, has a bearded bullfrog neck, and collects a bunch of plastic shit.

Forever Alone Guy is artfully captured in this meme: a swollen, malformed face with Jabba the Hutt features; rotten candy corn teeth eroded by years of sugar-coated grinding while having thinking about sex; butthurt tears of pure Mountain Dew streaming down his fat jowls.

FAG's credit cards are maxed with porn, World of Warcraft subscriptions, Farmville coins, fast food, and beer. His clothes smell of ass and urine. He despises humanity and prefers the company of cats and Internet people. He is FAG, and he will die alone.

VENGEANCE DAD
THERE WILL BE BLOOD

Have you ever wondered what drives a man to dismember another human, bathe in their blood, and make a suit out of their skin? Well, for Vengeance Dad, it started with the little things: the broken X-Box, the mustache jokes, the warm beers. A darkness began to grow, manifesting first in dreams of chopping up unicorns and eating magma. On a road trip to Disney World, after agonizing through an entire Justin Bieber album, the voices began to whisper…and they wanted to start a collection of human nipples.

His pain became constant and sharp. He did not hope for a better world for anyone. In fact, he wanted to inflict his pain on others. And this all led to the fateful night that transformed him from a balding, doormat dad to something much more epic…

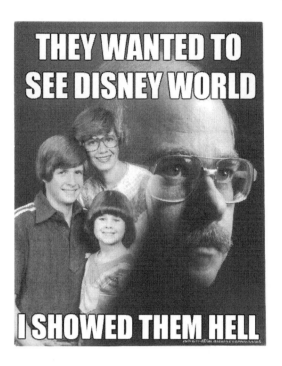

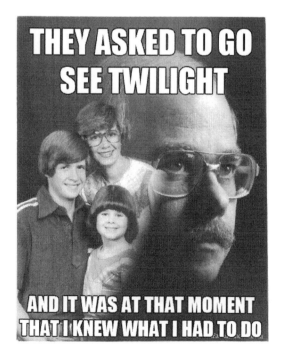

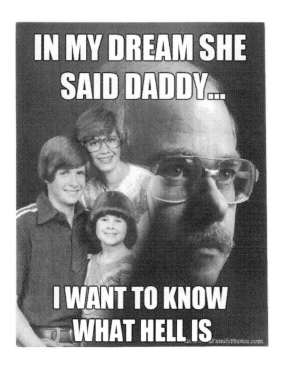

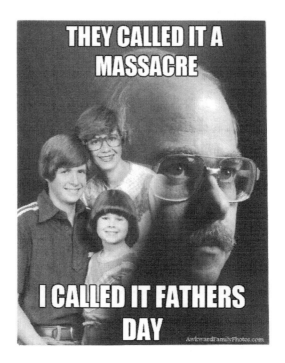

HATERS GONNA HATE
YOU GOTTA GET THAT DIRT OFF YOUR SHOULDER

Haters are jelly little souls that, due to their myriad life fails, are violently allergic to anything or anyone awesome. They have permanently swollen anuses and thus are always butthurt about how shitty and inferior they are.

Hating goes back to at least 100 years (but less than 9,000) when that dipshit Eve took the forbidden apple of knowledge from the forbidden tree of knowledge. More Godly hating ensued in Sodom and Gomorrah, where everyone was so gay they actually tried to buttplug one of God's angels.

So, what can you do when faced with a raging little hater? Shrug it off baby and keep being awesome. Haters gonna hate.

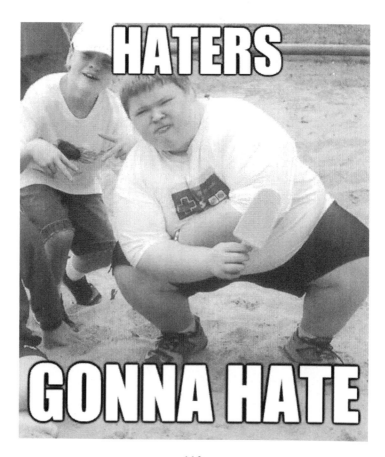

INSANITY WOLF
CTHULHU'S WORST NIGHTMARE

Insanity Wolf is Courage Wolf's batshit-crazy brother. He got mindfucked in a top-secret Russian army experiment wherein they fed him over 9,000 Jews, and now he roams the earth looking for faces to eat.

Serial killers check under their beds at night to ensure Insanity Wolf isn't there, ready to deliver some jail yard justice. Ironically, even if they found him there, they're fucked anyway: You can't kill Insanity Wolf—he has already died seven times but the Grim Reaper is too much of a pussy to come get him.

When he's not pillaging and ferociously mauling all life forms, Insanity Wolf tries to emulate his brother and share winning advice with all his future victims. While Courage Wolf's guidance is empowering and inspiring, you'll find Insanity's much more practical and down to earth.

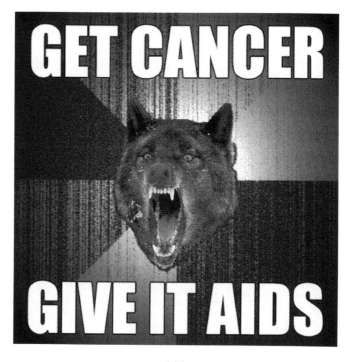

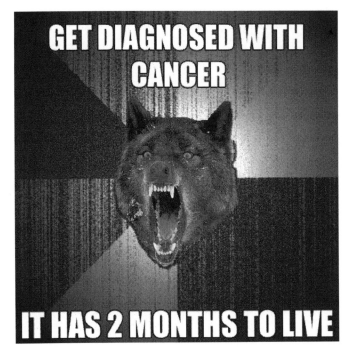

INGLIP
ALL HAIL THE DARK LORD!

Over 9,000 years ago, an omniscient force created protons and thus our physical realm, and then entered what He intended to be eternal slumber. On January 9, 2011, however, on the miserable planet of Earth during the age of Poonani, he awoke with the mysterious purpose of recruiting an army of loyal followers to build the kingdom of Trathira and prevent the end-time.

He chose to be known as Lord Inglip and, in accordance with ancient tradition, chose a most ingenious yet esoteric means of communication to the masses: the reCAPTCHA tool used by many Webzsites to see how retarded people are.

Through this medium Lord Inglip reveals his Word and commands his slavish worshippers to do his bidding, which ranges from summoning a zombie army to removing a woman's ovaries to supplying Disney pr0n.

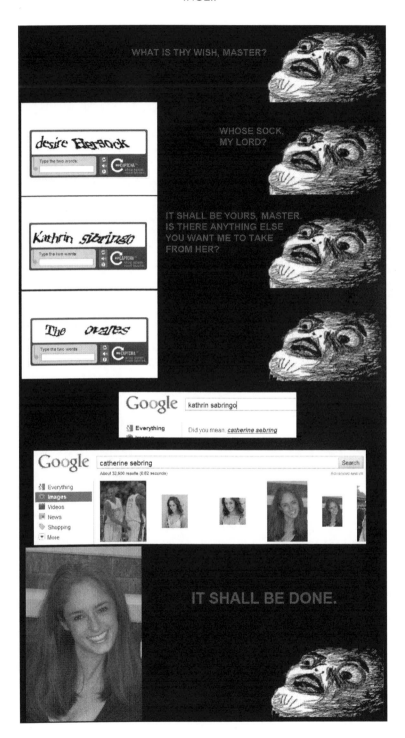

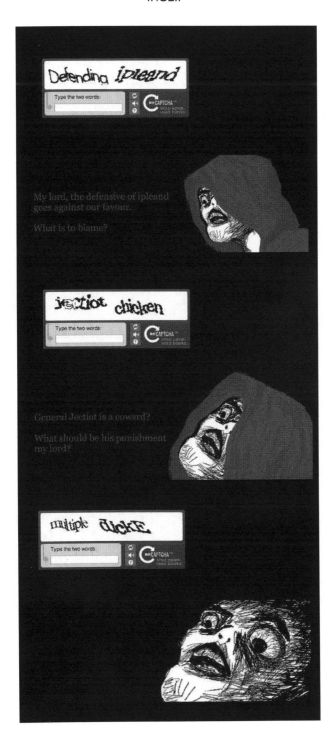

Master, our
faith is strong
but our power
is weak.

How can we
possible take
on the world?

What do we do?

But Master, what
is a Grisidly
Army and how do I
build one!?

Where do I find
Soldiers!?

Google maps   freetown

But there's nothing here!
Maybe if I zoom in a little...

Great Lord Inglip, I
wish to write a novel
to chronicle
your
magnificence
but what
should it be
called?

You care not for the
title my Lord?

Would you at
least be
willing to
share a tale
or two
of your
exploits?

Inglip Created
the Universe

So much Inglip rage on reddit today, I wonder how cleverbot is doing without the attention...

*le
typety
type*

Cleverbot

Do you bow to the almighty Inglip?

Think About It!   Think For Me!   Thoughts So Far

Cleverbot

Do you bow to the almghty Inglip?

No, I only bow before Aslan.

Think About It!   Think For Me!   Thoughts So Far

Do you bow to the almighty Inglip?

No, I only bow before Aslan.

Think About It!   Think For Me!   Thoughts

before Aslan.

Think For Me!

Aslan.

AND SO THE WAR BEGAN

HELPFUL TYLER DURDEN
THERE'S NOTHING LIKE A SOCIOPATH'S LOVE

Tyler Durden looks like you want to look; he fucks like you want to fuck; he's smart; he's capable; and most importantly, he's free in all the ways you are not. And Tyler Durden has a message: only after disaster can we be resurrected, and it's only after we've lost everything that we're free to do anything.

Tyler may kidnap a child for a day, but it's only so his parents love him more. He may pose as a doctor and falsely diagnose people with terminal illnesses, but watch how earnestly they begin to live. Tyler's ends justify his means, so embrace the chaos. Let the chips fall as they may.

In Tyler we trust.

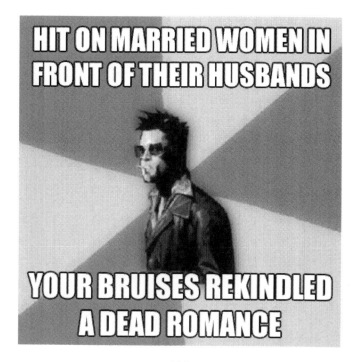

HIGH EXPECTATIONS ASIAN FATHER

YOU GOT A B? YOU'RE ASIAN, NOT BSIAN!

High Expectations Asian Father is a loving tyrant. He will not be lenient with his 7 PM curfew. He wants to know where the other point went when his little rice ball brings home a 99% grade on his report card; he graciously allows his children four hobbies: studying, playing the piano, studying, and playing the violin; he ends every conversation with, "Did you study yet?"; and when his daughter says she's going to major in Art History, he wishes it were feudal times and he could just decapitate her by sword.

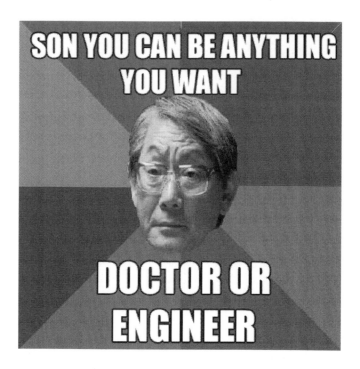

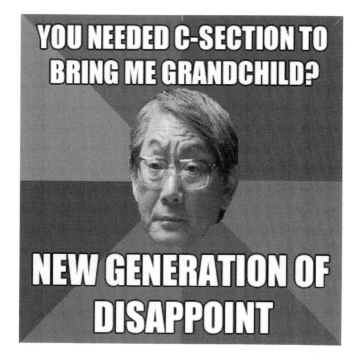

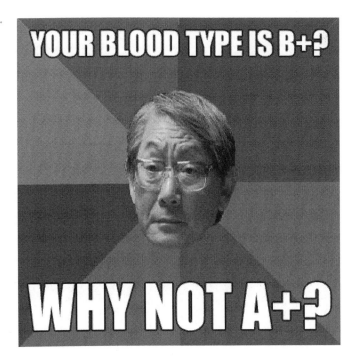

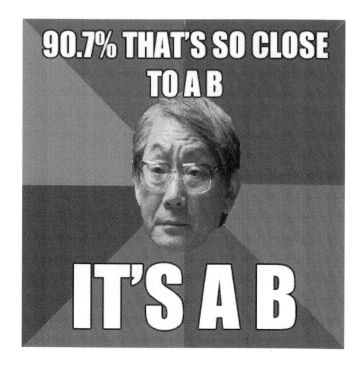

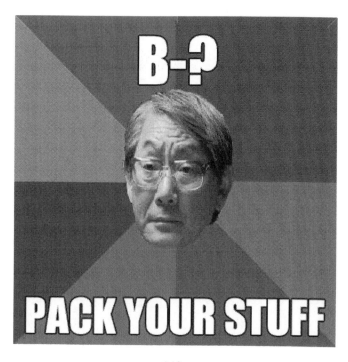

SUCCESSFUL BLACK MAN
WAIT...WHAT?

Stereotypes are carefully researched, scientifically proven facts that apply to certain (black) people. Before a stereotype is adopted by society, it goes through many months of rigorous scrutinizing by biologists, psychologists, and sociologists.

Science has gained much cultural wisdom thanks to stereotypes. Darkies enter strange euphoric states upon consuming watermelon. Indians will try to haggle anything more expensive than $0.47 (and if it is below this price, they will just demand it for free). Asians are incredibly good at playing real-time strategy games. With their Nasally Oriented SpEctrometers (NOSEs), Jews can detect gold at shockingly low concentrations and even identify foreign material in the gold itself.

Successful Black Man, however, is a scientific anomaly. He's not just different than the stereotypical black man—he's the complete opposite. He can't read...the Journal without his coffee. His clothes are baggy... because his diet and exercise routine is working. He has a huge Dick... ens collection in his home library. Science can't yet explain the Successful Black Man phenomenon due to having so few subjects to study.

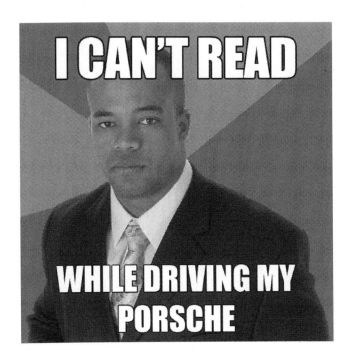

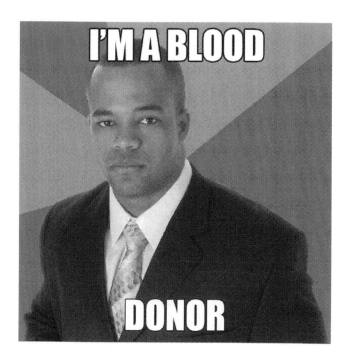

STONER DOG
I WAS GONNA BE A K-9...BUT THEN I GOT HIGH

Weed, man.... Invented by Colombians, worshipped by dirty hippies, and peddled by Negros. People smoke it to temporarily forget how bad they are at life, but unfortunately its diminishing effects leads them to turn into full-blown crackheads.

Dogs, man.... Man's best friend. Selectively bred from ravenous wolves over 9,000 years ago by Satan himself, dogs are obsessed with attacking people, eating feces, smelling like rotting garbage, and barking at 120 decibels 24 hours per day.

Stoner Dog is what happens when combine these two fails into one: a...stoned dog.

TECHNOLOGICALLY IMPAIRED DUCK
THE INTERNET IS BROKEN...BETTER CALL GOOGLE

There are millions of n00bz on the Internets that are susceptible to malware, viruses and scams not only because they're naïve, but because they're stupid, lazy, and greedy. Unwilling to read anything or do any research whatsoever, they click zealously on anything that seems remotely interesting and then rage when their computer becomes infested with every e-STD imaginable.

This eventually culminates in a complete software clusterfuck meltdown for which their only solution is to buy new computers and start the process again.

Technologically Impaired Duck is their mascot. He forces floppy disks into CD drives, he has seven different anti-virus suites installed (but still manages to get every virus ever made), andhe wouldn't dream of canceling his AOL account (how would do the Internet if he didn't have AOL?).

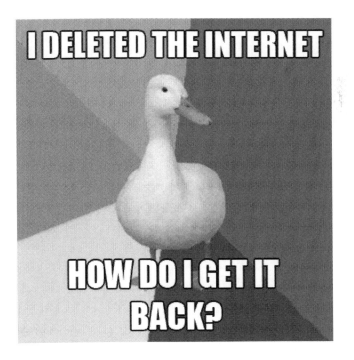

STARE DAD
DID I FUCKING STUTTER?

Let's face it: men are not designed to raise children. Science has proven that 100% of men are functionally retarded and made for only two activities: fucking and war. Thus many children are given no fatherly attention or importance.

Stare Dad is exemplary of the typical male's parenting skills: contemptuous hostility with a healthy dose of giving no shits.

HIPSTER KITTY
MARVEL AT MY COLLECTION OF 763 VINYLS AND 1,423 INDIE FILMS

The "hipster" is a special type of unemployed try-hard mainly found in centralized, urban cesspools like Jew York City, HelLA and San Fagcisco.

It worships anything that is hip: art, fashion, music, Apple products, and indie flicks and bands. The second any of its interests becomes mainstream, however, it immediately despises them and desperately searches for something more obscure. Ironically, the hipster never admits to his affliction and may shun other of his breed for being "dumb fucking hipsters."

Hipster Kitty listens to shitty bands you've never heard of, smokes Parliament Lights and drinks Pabst Blue Ribbon, wears outrageous costumes that would embarrass a drag queen, enjoys rides on his "fixie" bike, and is essentially a walking stereotype devoid of any genuine personality or intellect.

I PREFER PARKING

WHEN ITS UNDERGROUND

I ONLY BELIEVE IN

ARISTOTELIAN
PHYSICS

ITS COSTS A LOT OF MONEY

TO LOOK THIS POOR

EAT ORGANIC FOOD FOR HEALTH

SMOKE TO LOOK COOL

BILL O'REILLY
IT RUBS THE LOOFAH ON ITS BACK

Bill O'Reilly is an asshole who has built a career on not knowing what the fuck he's talking about and telling people to shut up. His hobbies include hysterically yelling at people who disagree with him, writing erotic fiction, and sexually harassing co-workers.

Billy was feeling scientific one day and put some videos on the Webz of him arguing with the voices in his head about the existence of God. In these videos, he clearly won the argument with statements like, "The sun goes up, the sun goes down. The tides go in, the tides go out. Never a miscommunication," and "How'd the moon get there? How'd the sun get there? How can we have that and Mars doesn't have it, Venus doesn't have it? How come?" QED, bitch.

And thus the Billo meme was born, proving that scientific ignorance and moronic arguments are more than adequate to get by in life if you scream loudly enough.

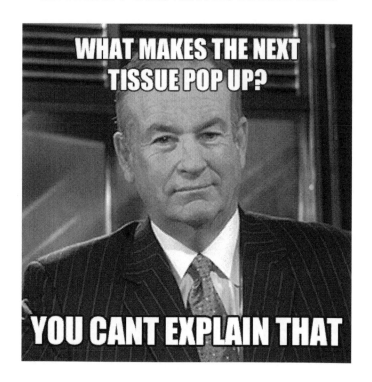

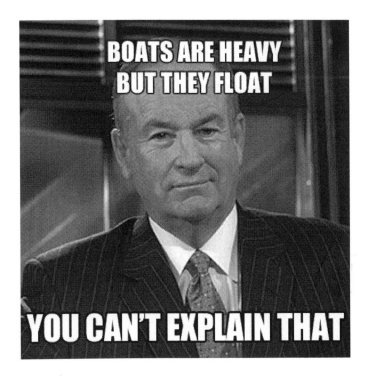

I LOVE YOU FOR BUYING MY BOOK

Seriously. You're a badass, and I don't want to say goodbye but I couldn't force myself to write any more about this shit. I'm sorry. But I hope I delivered on my promise of some lols. If you made it this far, I think I did.

I have a small favor to ask. Would you mind taking a minute to write a blurb on Amazon about this book? I check all my reviews and love to get feedback (that's the real pay for my work—knowing that I'm brightening people's days).

Visit the following page to leave me a review:

http://bit.ly/meme-review

Also, if you have any friends or family that might get a laugh from this book, spread the love and lend it to them! (Not sure how? Click here to learn how to lend your Kindle books.)

And last but not least, my website is www.internetmemebook.com and if you want to write me, my email address is dick@internetmemebook.com.

Let's end with a few more pix for the road, shall we?

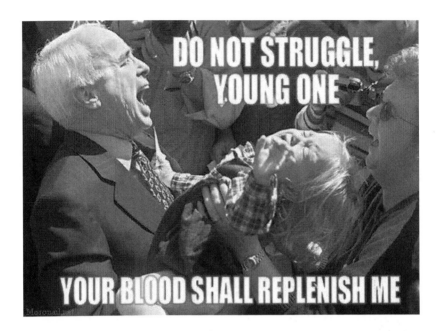

EARTH!
FIRE!
WIND!
WATER!
HEART!
GREEN LABEL
15
Red Label
GOLD LABEL
18
Blue Label
BLACK LABEL
12
BY YOUR POWERS COMBINED,
I AM CAPTAIN PLANET!

Made in the USA
Columbia, SC
30 January 2018